Be Interview-Wise
How to Prepare for and Manage Your Interviews

"Baada ya kisa, Mkasa — Baada ya chango, Kitendo"
"After a reason, a happening — After a thought — action."

Tippu Tip (1837-1905)

Brian McIvor

© 2008 Brian McIvor
ISBN 0-9519738-4-3
ISBN 978-0-9519738-4-4

All design, art work and liaison with printers has been undertaken by
Neworld Associates, 9 Greenmount Avenue, Harold's Cross, Dublin 12.

Publisher: Managements Briefs, 30 The Palms, Clonskeagh, Dublin 14.

Introduction

Why this book was written

Most people are terrified of being interviewed for a job or a promotion. Over the last 30 years in training I have met many people who said that they would prefer not ho have to undergo another interview. When I asked them why this was so I was told stories of being badly interviewed, bullied and being tricked at interviews. A substantial body of case law internationally shows that there is a lot of truth in this assertion. However, I also discovered that most people who had bad experiences of interviews had very little recollection of exactly what happened at their interview, and, most had not prepared properly. Also, many were terrified of further rejection if they went through with another interview.

This book is written for those who have had such experiences and for those who want to avoid painful and unproductive interviews. This book is also written for those super-heroes and heroines who were first in all their exams and competitions — whose interviews will be merely formalities. Or will they? I have also met many people who were baffled or hurt because,

despite their qualifications and experience they lost out to other candidates — and felt cheated as a result.

In the 21st century where people will change jobs far more frequently than any previous generation resumés will have to be kept up to date and interview skills will have to be honed to ensure constant employment and employability.

This book was written to help you prepare, handle and review your next interview — whether it be your first interview for your first job, a job change or a promotional interview. Traditional techniques of interviewing are covered in the book and special emphasis is placed on more recent approaches — including competency interviews and making presentations to an interview panel/board.

Bookstores have many books dealing with interviewing — normally the format is "Your answers to the 100 toughest interview questions". Although some of these are useful in a limited way they are generic in their nature. This book only deals with 10 generic questions – but they cover the main areas! You can waste considerable amounts of time trying to master prepared answers to long lists of contrived questions. This time could be better put to use researching the job and organisation you are interested in.

Your objective at the interview is to help the interview panel (or Interviewer) match the job description to your ability to do the job – as proven by you during the interview. The interview is a structured conversation with a specific purpose – and possibly your first meeting with your future boss. The interview is a complex process –containing elements of a trial (search for evidence and proof), group therapy (dealing with feelings) and a business negotiation (buying expertise and skills). You need to be aware of these elements and many others to make the process a successful one.

Table of Contents

Acknowledgements

I owe a huge debt to a number of people:

Andrew McLaughlin of the Irish Management Institute, with whom I have worked over many years in training both Interviewers and Interviewees and in preparing various materials including texts, videotapes and DVDs. Andrew has also been an inspirational guide in introducing me to the techniques of rapport and non-verbal communication. Andrew also developed the EPOLA framework referred to in Chapter 3.

Mary Hanson, Human Resources Consultant, who has worked with me on various interviewing programmes and video projects since our days in the Institute of Public Administration. She contributed material on dress code in Chapter 6.

Martin Farrelly, latterly of the Irish Management Institute with whom I also worked with on programmes and who shared his insights into practical HR matters.

Richard Nelson Bolles (USA), author of '*What Color is your Parachute?*' for his support and wisdom but also his unique insights into skills identification as the starting point for career decision making, and by extension the process of job matching.

Frank Scott-Lennon for his on-going support and editorial influence; also for contributing the LIP insight and mnemonic within Chapter 4.

Kevin O'Kelly for his insight into the spiritual nature of work.

Gráinne Killeen for her encouragement and support in getting me started on writing this and other books.

Pat Ryan for her support and consistent clear thinking.

Brian McIvor
December 2008

Some Very Basic Questions

Chapter outline
Some Very Basic Questions

→   Interviews are complex

→   Where is my career going?

→   What chance do I really have?

→   Why have my previous interviews failed?

→   Do I know what makes me an effective
    performer at interview?

→   What is the Interviewer really looking for?

→   What will I get out of the interview —
    whatever the result?

Introduction

It is flattering at the end of a job search to get an invitation to be interviewed. However, you need to be realistic about your chances if called to interview. Should I be doing this interview if the job does not really suit me? Most Interviewees prepare very badly for interview. The most frequent error is to underestimate the nature and depth of the interview. For a critical interview you will need up to 30 hours preparation — which will include preparing and refining the Curriculum Vitae, researching the position and building up your case for the job in question.

Interviews are complex

The basic definition of a job interview is that it is a structured conversation with the purpose of matching the individual to the job. However, the interview is far more complex than that.

It is said that a typical recruitment interview is a cross between a court of law, group therapy and a high-level business deal negotiation.

The job interview is like a court of law – Facts have to be established and a case has to be made. There are rules and regulations governing what is and is not admissible. There is no place for hearsay or speculation. At the end of the day a judgment is made which has a good chance of being the wrong one, if essential evidence is omitted or if what is presented is misinterpreted. There is also the prospect of a life sentence if the wrong person is matched to the wrong job and if the employer and employee have to live with the consequences of poor performance and lack of job satisfaction. It has been well-established internationally that one in two people are in the wrong job. An interview that fails to match the right candidate to the right job to the benefit of both is partly to blame. A substantial part of the blame also attaches to many candidates offering themselves for the wrong job or others who are ill-prepared and ill-informed about the nature of the job they are going for. This happens particularly with promotions where the Interviewee's focus is on progression and a better salary rather than the demands of the job and their ability to match them.

It is said that a typical recruitment interview is a cross between a court of law, group therapy and a high-level business deal negotiation.

The job interview as group therapy – Interviews involve people in situations where rapport has to be established quickly and effectively. Chemistry between Interviewer and Interviewee is crucial and there are many potential biases in the process. The main one is the tendency of both parties to judge each other prematurely. For the Interviewer the danger is in deciding prematurely that the candidate is suitable or otherwise and having this decision consciously or unconsciously affect their subsequent line of questioning. For Interviewees the tendency is to jump to conclusions prematurely and to misjudge the Interviewers'

4

reactions (or lack of them) to their answers. What is said is one dimension of the interview, but people communicate very powerfully in non-verbal ways — by providing or withdrawing support — in subtle ways. Verbatim transcripts of interviews do not give the full flavour of what really happened at an interview.

The job interview as a business deal negotiation — An interview may be the start of a contractual process between an individual and an organisation that may involve very large amounts of money. A yardstick in human resources is that a bad hire costs a company at least one and a half years salary. For the Interviewee

---

Panel 1.1

Imagine the last time you saw a really interesting interview on television — one where you got the sense that the Interviewer was 'onto something' and probed accordingly.

What did the Interviewer do?

---

1 They researched the background to the interview and had a clear understanding of what information they wanted and of the issues that might be covered

2 They set the scene

3 Put the Interviewee at ease by creating rapport and trust

4 Listened very carefully to the Interviewee's answers

5 Made sure the answers were relevant to the subject of the interview

6 Summarised what they heard

7 Asked the Interviewee to be more concise, or to summarise

8 Probed the data and tested the logic

9 Looked for gaps (or half-truths!)

10 Challenged woolly answers

11 Managed the time frame carefully and wrapped it up at the end

12 Let the viewers know what was going to happen next

This is exactly what happens in job interviews!

the deal is a meal ticket — possibly for life — to the value of a typical lottery prize (check the maths!). The nice part is that you are more likely to win the job lottery than the state one — but most people refuse to put in the work to make the deal happen. The organisation is also trying to hire the right person at the right price so the Interviewee has to be conscious of their correct value in the marketplace. Human Resource departments have the advantage in this area because of their access to salary surveys. The result is that an excellent candidate can lose out because the price was not right.

Where is my Career going?

To put that into context you will need to have a clear understanding of the following:

What is the state of your career at the moment?

→ On the way up, at a plateau etc.)

What is your Ultimate Career Goal?

→ Level

→ Salary

→ Type of work you would like to be doing

What will help me get there:

→ What do I need to organise (training, development, experience etc.) to get me there?

The exercises within the Workbook Supplement at the end of this book will be helpful in focusing your mind on questions such as the above.

Are you in the right job?

Many people find themselves in the wrong job — a 2008 survey of the UK workforce found that 24 per cent or one in four are not satisfied with their job — and almost one in three (30 per cent) do not feel engaged by their employer, according to a report from the TUC.

Before you present yourself for interview — will the job you are applying for make you one of the 24% — just because the money or prospects are better?

What chance do I really have?

Have I considered the field for this job?

Ⓐ Am I a front runner?

Ⓑ In the middle of the pack?

Ⓒ At the back?

If your answer is **A** your objective is to ensure you are number 1 and you don't do anything to jeopardise your chances

If your answer is **B** you can increase your chances dramatically by researching the job and the interview process. Research shows that you can put yourself into the front by understanding as much as you can about how the interview and recruitment process you are engaging in works.

If your answer is **C** you need to ask yourself seriously *why am I doing this?* You could be putting yourself under serious stress and, even worse, undermining your performance at subsequent interviews. However, you may decide to do the interview anyway – to get practice. Sometimes this confident attitude can actually get you the job!

Why have previous interviews failed?

The challenge for you is to understand why you did not succeed previously. The standard excuses are:

→ The board made a mistake and hired the wrong person

→ I was too nervous on the day

→ The decision was made already

→ I don't like talking about myself

→ I am an introvert and they always hire extroverts

→ I am too old, too expensive, nobody wants me

The last point might get this reaction: *who would want to hire anyone who went into a job interview with a poor attitude like that?*

There are other reasons you should consider in reviewing past failures in a constructive way:

→ You qualified in the top three – but the successful candidate had something in particular that the company wanted

→ You would have got the job but you did not do enough preparation – *and you knew that in your heart of hearts*

→ You lacked confidence going into the interview and communicated this very successfully to the Interviewer(s)

→ You did not engage properly with the board. You did not listen properly to questions and the data you supplied was not relevant

→ The Interviewer(s) were biased in some way – which was not your fault

→ You were unrealistic in your salary expectations

The challenge for you is to put previous experiences into perspective, get relevant feedback (if you can) and acquire professional Interviewee skills.

Do I know what makes me an effective performer at interview?

While most Interviewees are only too aware of their faults as Interviewees — very few people know where they score in their interviews — unless they have taken time out to examine their technique outside of the real interview. Interview boards register differences between variations in your performance. In an interview most people should be able to do the following without too much trouble:

→ Explain the main parts of your current job

→ Describe what your company/department does

→ Describe your company's products or services

→ Talk about themselves, in general terms

→ Talk about your record and experiences to date

Other areas where you may have done well at the interview, without realising it might have been:

→ Describing projects you enjoyed

→ Discussing the challenges of your current role and how you perform

→ Points where you established good rapport with your Interviewers

→ Points in the interview where you scored points (Interviewers won't let you know this!)

→ Product and service descriptions

The challenge is for you to think about yourself in positive and constructive ways. If you can honestly describe your attitude as open, positive and enthusiastic the chances are that this impression will have been made in the interview.

If all else fails ask yourself these two questions:

❶ What got me my first job?

❷ What got me noticed, promoted?

Review feedback from others in your recent past to help you build up a reliable picture of how you present to others.

Panel 1.2

Research shows that the main reasons Interviewees fail at interviews include the following:

→ Not having a clear understanding what the job is and how their knowledge, skills and experience is related to the performance requirements of the job being filled.

→ Not listening properly to the questions being asked or engaging in a real exchange with the Interviewers

→ Long irrelevant answers

→ Not being properly prepared

→ Lack of experience in being interviewed

→ Lying or mis-representing information to the Interviewer

→ Interviewees focus on the what the job will do for them rather than what they will contribute to the company

→ Woolly language, bad communication

→ Poor presentation, body language and rapport.

→ Bias (unconscious or conscious) on the part of the Interviewers (e.g. picking people they like and can identify with — rather than thinking through what the company really needs).

What is the Interviewer really looking for?

Interview boards want to know:

→ If you know what the job involves — what are the results expected?

→ If you are able to do the job — do you have the skills, attributes and knowledge required?

→ If you are willing to do the job — and to grow in the role over time

→ If you can fit in with your colleagues and the culture of the organisation

Numerous studies have shown that organisational fit is the most important of these. As levels of education improve it is more difficult to distinguish between candidates on the basis of their qualification. Organisational fit can be tested (in a limited way) during the interview by the quality of rapport between Interviewee and board although this can be the subject of bias.

And can you prove it by the following:

→ Your evidence of the results you have achieved in the past

→ Your ability to communicate well and answer questions in depth during the interview

→ Your ability to analyse data quickly

→ Your ability to demonstrate what you have learned as a result of experience

→ By creating good rapport and contact during the interview

What will I get out of the interview – whatever the result?

You may have assessed your chances at the interview and concluded that you are not really in the running. The decision to do the interview is then up to you. Here are a number of good reasons why you should undergo the interview anyway:

❶ You will get practice in being interviewed outside your comfort zone

❷ It may bring you to the notice of the company – who may contact you subsequently, if they are sufficiently impressed

❸ You will get a chance to benchmark yourself against others – particularly useful in the case of promotion interviews

❹ Your Interviewers may be offering feedback later – which may help you to get other jobs

If all else fails ask yourself these two questions:

If you have experience doing company presentations you can recycle such items as:

ACTIVITY:
Answering the Basic Questions

See the Workbook Supplement at the end of the book.

⮕ Take time out to examine your reasons for doing the job interview and how it will help advance your career by completing Exercise 1.

Summary of Chapter 1

→ Review your career plans before you do an interview — ask yourself is this a good move?

→ Rate yourself against the competition — realistically

→ Examine your previous experience with interviews constructively

→ Interviewers and Interviewees are poor at recalling what happens at interviews — get good data on your performance

→ Be clear on what you want the interview to achieve for you — what are the messages and impressions you want to leave

→ Interviewers are looking for knowledge of the job, the ability to do it, proof that you have done something similar before and that you will fit in well in their organisation — especially the latter.

2

Preparing for the Interview

Chapter outline
Preparing for the Interview

→ How the Interviewer prepares
→ How the Interviewee prepares
→ Helping the HR Department help you
→ Promotion Interviews

Introduction

Interviewers spend a lot of time preparing for the job interview — shouldn't you? What you are preparing for should be a professional conversation the objective of which is to match you to the job. Many people do not take the interview seriously — seeing it as something that has to be gone through — like some form of arcane ritual. Others feel the need to oversell themselves and look for ways to put themselves top of the list — even if that involves a bit of lying and misrepresentation. Such an approach is fatal in any interview situation as it destroys trust and your perceived credibility.

How the Interviewer prepares

→ Writing Job descriptions and Person Specifications

→ Reviewing performance of previous job-holders

→ Future-proofing the job

→ Screening CVs and Letters of Application

How the Interviewee prepares

→ Review the Job

→ Identify the Essential and Desirable Skills, Knowledge and Attributes required

→ Establish how you will prove your suitability

→ Compare the data (forms, CVs, Letters)

→ Plan the Interview, Questions, Replies to Questions, Dealing with Gaps.

Not much difference is there?

Research proves that...

You can improve your chances of success by understanding as much as possible about how the interviewing process operates. Successful candidates think about the job in a similar way to the Interviewer and focus on the question – if I were the Interviewer what would I be looking for? It is better to think of the interview as a collaborative process than an adversarial one.

How the Interviewer prepares

Writing Job Descriptions and Person Specifications

A key part of the interview preparation is the writing of the **job description** and the **person specification.** These are two separate tasks, as one focuses on the results required and the other focuses on the knowledge, skills and attributes of the job-holder.

⮞ The job description:

The main components are:

→ Job objective

→ Principal responsibilities of the job

→ Reporting Relationship(s)

> Letters of Application and CVs are screened on the basis of how well they demonstrate the competencies that the job requires.

⮞ The person specification:

The main components are:

→ Experience required

→ Qualifications required

→ Competencies or Skills required

→ Behaviours of effective holders of the job

→ Negative indicators (e.g. lack of consideration for colleagues, customer etc.)

→ Attitudes, attributes required

To be successful at the interview you need to have an in-depth understanding of both of the above and how you can fully understand the job and what the Interviewers will be looking for.

Reviewing performance of previous job-holders

If the job you are applying for is an internal promotion or a job that is not a unique one it is important to realise that Interviewers will have reviewed current holders of the job to identify any deficiencies that any new applicants must not have. A common mistake with internal promotions is to assume that you are stepping into the shoes of the previous holder — this is particularly true if the previous holder has been in place for a number of years. If they have been too long in the job you can expect that expectations will be greater for whoever steps into their place.

Future-proofing the job

A Human Resources professional will also look at the impact of company strategy and developments in future-proofing a job. If markets are to expand or contract the job will need to allow for future, but as yet unspecified, demands.

Many jobs are created following strategic reviews as the organisation strives to match resources with a new or revised direction.

Put Yourself in the HR Department's shoes!

Consider the situation: You work in the HR department – you have 100 CVs to screen and you are working late. You come across one that is difficult to relate to the job you are trying to fill, it looks 'off the peg' as if it had been sent in for other jobs. There are a number of typos and the typeface is difficult to read. What will you do with this annoying CV? **This could be _your_ precious CV!**

Screening CVs and Letters of Application

Human Resource Departments screen job applications on the basis of the minimum acceptable standard as outlined in the job description or advertisement. If the number of applicants is large there may be a rigorous screening stage. To survive this your application should clearly show that you meet the basic requirements or better. People who screen your Curriculum Vitae will also be influenced by the quality of presentation and how easy it is to readily access the data therein. CVs may be excluded because of glaring mistakes or carelessness in presentation.

Letters of Application and CVs are screened on the basis of how well they demonstrate the competencies that the job requires. If you are applying your emphasis should be on showing how your skills, experience and knowledge are relevant to the job in question.

How the Interviewee prepares for the Interview

Researching the Job

It is essential to research your job thoroughly under the following headings:

→ What results are expected from the holder?

→ How does the job fit into the work of their department/company?

→ What is the company profile?

→ What is happening in that sector/industry at present?

→ What are future trends or threats in that industry?

→ What is the market share/perception of this company in the marketplace?

→ How are their products/services regarded in the marketplace?

→ How much product development does the company do?

If you are applying to a company you do not know well you will need to consult the following:

→ Company website for a copy of their strategy statement, annual results

→ Other websites for news stories relevant to the company e.g. are they going out of business?

→ Customer satisfaction surveys

→ Publications in the standard guides and references in your local library

→ Previous job holders or people in similar positions in related fields

Matching your application to the job

Armed with the job description, the person specification and your Curriculum Vitae try, to relate one to another.

Do the experience, skills and achievements being looked for in the job stand out in your CV?

Become completely familiar with all three documents so that you can help bring the Interviewers to the conclusion that you are the person for the job.

Panel 2.3

Hints for gathering data on an organisation:

● **HINT:** Try engaging with the company as a customer so that you can get a first-hand experience of how their systems work

→ You may get first hand experience of what the company is like to work for!

→ Observe what happens if you present a detailed technical question or a non-standard situation. You may see first-hand how staff are managed (or not!)

→ It is better to be a frustrated customer than a frustrated employee. Keep asking the question – does this look like a good place to work?

→ It is easier to move your custom than change your job!

→ You may also be gathering valuable information for the interview; companies are frequently curious about what people really think about them or what really happens to their customers

Panel 2.3

Hints for relating your CV to the job:

❶ Give the documentation to someone else to read. Give them the job description and ask them to compare the two. Watch their puzzled expression!

❷ Be so familiar with your own CV/Application that you can tell what the Interviewer is reading from across a table and upside down! Try this with a friend

❸ Consider bringing a revised CV to the interview if you think that the original one was deficient

ACTIVITY:

At this stage of preparation it may be helpful for you to complete Exercises 1, 3 and 4 within the Workbook Supplement at the back of the book; these exercises focus on your recent work experience and the skills and competencies that you have acquired.

Helping the HR Department to help you

Spend time tailoring the CV to the job — check how easy it is to find proof of the job requirements in your documentation. If you are writing a letter of application — show first that you understand what the job is asking for.

Provide proof from your experience that you have what it takes. Most CVs are produced in the default format of the applicant's word processor and are thus unsuitable and no different from most CVs that will be seen. Make yours different by using a readable, clear typeface and by making it easy to process.

Promotion Interviews

If you are going for an internal promotion in your organisation you will need to prepare well and in depth. The danger is that there may be pre-conceived ideas by your colleagues about your performance. The interview can give you a positive opportunity to set the record straight. Go back to the basic questions:

❶ When you joined the company: What got you appointed? Why not the other 100 people who applied at the same time?

❷ What got you promoted previously?

Review your performance over the last two or three years. Remind yourself of successful projects. Bring yourself up to speed on what you achieved and how you achieved it.

Examine your performance reviews in detail to understand what elements of your performance were valued and rewarded in your current role. Consider how your job relates to other roles in your team and how your efforts support your colleagues and those above you. A good definition of a member of staff is someone you can rely on.

A useful exercise is to review the support that you provide for other people by identifying:

→ What people rely on you in some way?

→ What do they rely on you for?

→ What skills/expertise are you using in supporting them?

We will now turn in chapter 3 to the important issue of Interview Structure.

ACTIVITY:

See exercise 6 within the Workbook Supplement at the end of the book.

AISHA's Dilemma:
My boss is on my promotion interview board —
we have a difficult relationship — what do I do?

Aisha's situation is a common one. All she can do is to focus on providing the proof that the board require and answering the questions asked. In a real-life company situation such a difficult relationship may be also known to her colleagues who may be sympathetic to her situation. Interview boards have a legal requirement to be fair and to assess only the information that is presented to them. If she can be clear and objective during the interview she can do well. It is better, if you are in Aisha's situation, that you work from the assumption that your colleagues will act fairly.

Summary of Chapter 2

→ Interviewers and Interviewees should prepare in similar ways — your objective is to ensure that they see you have what they need to make the decision in your favour

→ Base your application on a marriage of the job description, job specification and your CV

→ Make the documentation as focussed and as user-friendly as possible for the people who will read it

→ Review your record of achievements and work done for the last year

→ For promotion interviews — look on it as an opportunity to put your case for the job and assume you will be treated fairly

3

Interview Structure

Chapter outline
Interview Structure

→ The Interview process
→ Traditional Interviews
→ Competency (Behavioural) Interviews
→ Mixed Interviews
→ Phone (Screening Interviews)

The Interview process

The job interview is sometimes defined as a structured conversation with a purpose.

For the Interviewer the purpose is to find the right candidate. For the Interviewee the purpose is to persuade the Interviewer that he/she is the best person for the job!

The danger for the Interviewer is to turn the conversation into an interrogation and to miss the right candidate in the process, by misinterpreting the data obtained under stress. As an Interviewee you need to avoid anticipating or experiencing the interview as an interrogation.

If the Interviewer and Interviewee together create mutual rapport and respect the result will be better disclosure on the Interviewee's part and better results on the Interviewer's part.

STAGES in the INTERVIEW PROCESS:

❶ The Traditional Interview

→ Introduction:
The purpose is for all the parties to be introduced, to establish initial rapport, and to explain **Purpose, Process, and Roles** of the interview. Use this opportunity to establish eye contact with your Interviewers

→ Initial Settling Questions: To get you talking and for the Interviewer to make an initial assessment of how the interview is going to go

→ Education and Qualifications: To confirm and explore details or gaps in the resumé (CV)

→ Work Experience: To check your abilities and knowledge

→ Duties of the job being offered: To see if your abilities and knowledge match the job

→ Salary Expectations: To check if the employer can afford you − but also to allow you to make a case for special treatment

→ Last Checks: To check if all the detail is complete

TRADITIONAL INTERVIEWS − Assess candidates under the following headings:

⮕ EDUCATION − Qualifications, Degrees, Certificates etc.

⮕ EXPERIENCE − Including Service Record

⮕ KNOWLEDGE − Professional and Sectoral, Current Events: National and World

⮕ **SPECIFIC APTITUDES** – Skills – Interpersonal, Analytical and Physical

⮕ **ATTRIBUTES or TRAITS** – Personality Type

⮕ **ATTAINMENTS** – Achievements and Awards

⮕ **SERVICE RECORD** – Including Promotion and Progression

⮕ **FIT FOR THE JOB** – Including membership of teams.

⮕ **GENERAL INTELLIGENCE**

⮕ **DISPOSITION** – Motivation, Attitude toward the job

⮕ **INTERESTS** – Useful as an indicator of motivation, ability to work well in teams (or otherwise) or to show skills that have not been used in the workplace but which might be useful on promotion (e.g. team leading and coaching skills in sport).

❷ The Competency or Behavioural Approach

Most interviews nowadays use some form of competency or behavioural approach. The term 'behavioural interviewing' is a more useful term because it focuses on evidence of past behaviours relevant to the job being filled. This type of interview is designed to identify your knowledge, competencies or skills that are of value to the organisation. Interviewing is based on finding examples of behaviours which are relevant to the job being filled. The core idea is that past behaviour is a reliable indicator of future performance – so the emphasis is on the identification and probing of historical examples of effective performance on the job. Typical examples would include: Leadership Skills, Financial Expertise or Change Management Skills.

> ⮕ **HINT:** You should be aware of the structure of a Competency Interview:

The classic competency interview does not explore your resumé (CV) or work experience chronologically but looks for core competencies which are key to success in the job being filled.

Each competency is identified in turn and you are then asked questions to establish the depth and breadth of your competence, what you achieved, what you learned and how you applied that learning later on.

A common formula that is used is called the **EPOLA** formula:

E – **Experience Objective**
P – **Probe Objective**
O – **Outcomes Objective**
L – **Learning Objective**
A – **Application Objective**

➡ Experience Objective:
To probe the breadth and depth of your experience.

Example: Can you tell me of a time when you used your leadership skills to best advantage?

➡ Probe Objective:
To present and explore a historic example of the competency.

Example: Tell me about a time when you had to use your initiative. Tell me what you did − step by step.

➡ Outcomes Objective:
To put figures on the results you achieved and to ensure that you are operating at the level appropriate to the job.

Example: What savings did the project deliver?

➡ Learnings Objective:
To identify how you use your experience to develop your skills.

Example: What new skills have you learned during your time in Sales?

➡ Application Objective:
To establish if you are proactive in carrying forward what you have learned.

Example: You said you did a computer diploma − what changes did you make to your systems as a result of what you had learned on the course?

Some misconceptions about Competency/behavioural interviewing:

ⓐ Interviews are only looking for one example of your competency

→ In the E stage above you may be asked to talk about the number of years experience and levels of your competencies. You may be asked to identify typical examples of the competency in action.

ⓑ One example can be used to cover several competencies

→ This looks like laziness on your part or lack of clarity as to what the competency is. Competencies are precisely defined − the job and competency descriptions should be examined in detail.

ⓒ Find somebody who has good examples and re-cycle them

→ Interviewers are trained to test if the example is particular to the individual. Expect questions about when, where and who else was involved.

ⓓ You can claim that because you worked in a team the achievement was the team's.

→ Interviewers understand how teams work and will explore

27

what your precise role was and the results that the team expected from you.

(e) Competency-based interviewing is a meaningless ritual – all competencies are generic. Competency-based interviewing, used properly, is a very powerful tool to match the individual to the job and is used to predict effective performance on the job. Nearly every organisation that has ever used it would not go back to the traditional way of doing things.

(f) Competency Interviews are now required by law There is no law that requires an interview to be conducted along competency lines. However, most countries now require interviews to be properly structured with the criteria and job descriptions being well defined. In some places the law requires that every candidate be asked exactly the same questions. Some HR professionals argue with justification that this discriminates against candidates because of differing communication styles (e.g. a shy or introverted candidate would need more direction than others).

Differences between traditional interviews and competency interviews are shown within the table opposite.

Two Useful Structures to help you handle Competency-based questions:

Many Interviewers use the **PAR** and **STAR** frameworks in competency interviewing.

PAR =
PROBLEM, ACTION and RESULT

P PROBLEM
→ **Question:** *Tell me about a problem you had with a difficult client.*
The Interviewer needs a concise definition of a problem you dealt with- keep it short!

A ACTION
→ **Question:** *What were the main actions you took?*
The Interviewer needs the main things you did. Focus on skills you used, problems you solved. Be very specific but do not get bogged down in detail.

R RESULT
→ **Question:** *What did you achieve?*
The Interviewer needs specifics: numbers, costs, yields, results.

STAR =
Situation, Task, Action and Result

As above except:

S SITUATION
→ You are asked to state the background to the situation concisely!

Differences between traditional interviews and competency interviews:

Focus	Traditional interviews focus on what you know and what your qualifications are	Competency interviews focus on what you know and what you have done
Structure	Traditional interviews tend to be less structured. The benefit was that this allowed Interviewers flexibility to explore	Competency interviews are highly structured, therefore precise answers are required
Questioning	A traditional Interviewer would tend to ask – *What would you do if?*	A competency Interviewer asks: *What did you do when?*
Communication Style	Traditional interviews explore your views about things	Competency interviews are less conversational than traditional interviews. There is a danger in thinking that rapport is not important in competency interviews. Because such interviews are highly structured does not mean that rapport is unimportant. Interviewers, like all human beings respond to engagement and good eye contact
Opinions	Important in traditional interviewing as your opinions were valuable in helping the Interviewer understand your motivation	Competency interviews avoid exploring views and feelings and focus on actions, results and applied learning
FIT to the JOB	Some traditional interviews could include questions which might test your ability to do jobs other than the one on offer	Competency interviews relate to the specific world of the job and not to general competence. Competency profiles of the job to be filled are used to generate the questions and the proofs expected in the interview

T TASK
→ You are asked to define the result you needed to achieve. Very similar to P in **PAR.**

A ACTION
→ As in PAR above

R RESULT
→ As in PAR above

NB Avoid the temptation to waste time in long stories.

How to help the Interviewer in Competency-based interviews:

❶ Keep it short and snappy. Competency-based interviews can take up to 50% more time than the traditional format. Long stories are out!

❷ Relate your examples as closely as you can to the job description and the competency definitions. Take time to match them

❸ Avoid using 'we'. Be very specific about what you did

❹ Relate your points to the competencies. For example: "I think my leadership skills were being tested here because the team had lost direction and were focussed on blaming each other. So what I did was to motivate them by…"

❺ Research the job. If the job is inside your own organisation find out the recent history and the challenges and demands of the position. This information would be used by the Interviewers in defining the competencies and framing the question. This could give you a very strong advantage! If it is in a company that you don't know research that sector.

Sample Competency Questions

An ability to work with people

→ Give an example of the range of working relationships you have with others

→ Which working relationships demand the most of your skills?

→ How do you deal with conflicting demands from people you work for?

To plan and prioritise

→ Give an example of where you had to prioritise your own work and that of others

→ Give an example of a project where you devised a plan, implemented it and reviewed it upon completion

To make decisions

→ How would you describe your decision-making style?

→ How does your way of making decisions differ from others?

→ What have you learned about decision making from your work?

Good communication skills

→ What is your range of communication skills?

→ Which communication skills are you most proficient at?

→ Give an example of where you had to present to a very senior group

→ How have you helped colleagues understand a complex work system?

→ What written guides have you produced for your staff or for members of the public?

Leadership Qualities

→ Give an example of where you had to lead others through a period of change

→ What leadership skills have you developed over the last few years?

→ How would others in your team describe your leadership style?

→ How would you help a member of your team become more proactive on the job?

Mixed Interviews

A more recent trend in interviewing is to provide an interview that has elements of both the traditional interview and the competency profile. In addition to being asked for evidence of previous performance you may be also asked the following:

→ How to deal with hypothetical situations that may arise on the job

→ Your knowledge of the company, its products and issues in its marketplace

→ Discuss controversial topics of a general nature (e.g. is our industry over-regulated?) or company specific (e.g. we do not allow our members to belong to a union, what is your view of this?) – this will be explored further in Chapter 4

→ To talk about yourself and your personality and to check if you will fit in

Many professionals feel that this approach gives an opportunity to get a more rounded picture of the Interviewee.

Telephone Interviews

It is normal practice to interview by phone at preliminary stages or for some jobs

→ Phone interviews are usually much shorter than face-to-face ones and are usually conducted by a junior member of staff

→ The Interviewer will usually have a very tightly constructed script in front of them – which will be based on the job description and the person specification

→ The interview may also be just a data collection exercise and the Interviewer may have little discretion in how it is to be conducted

→ The objective of a phone interview is to screen candidates for more in-depth interviews

→ Be sure to be very concise in your answers – take your time in answering the questions. The silence may give your Interviewer an opportunity to rescue you!

→ You can also have your resumé (CV) and the job application in front of you when you do it. This can help you control nerves and make a better impression!

→ Because you cannot see your Interviewer you will need to speak clearly. Use a warm tone of voice to build rapport. Listen to the tone and pace of their voice and try to match their style as much as possible without compromising your own.

ACTIVITY:
PARs and STARs

See exercises 7 and 8 within the Workbook Supplement at the end of the book.

➔ Take time out to describe some relevant work achievements using these structures. It will help you to help the Interviewer!

Summary of Chapter 3

→ Understand and anticipate the different types of interviews you may undergo

→ Structured interviews should be prepared for by researching your own experience and being prepared to be just as structured in your answers

→ Competency (behavioural) interviews are primarily focussed on your previous experience as the evidence to predict future performance

→ Interviews may be a mixture of traditional and competency questions

→ Phone interviews need to be focussed – but the big bonus is that you can have the documentation in front of you!

Managing Questions

4

Chapter outline
Managing Questions

→ Types of questions
→ How Interviewers can get it wrong!
→ Deep probing techniques
→ How long should an answer be?
→ Structuring your answers
→ Dealing with the 'opinion question'
→ Preparing for the ten standard questions

Introduction

You will need to be prepared for the various types of questions you may be asked during the interview. It can be a potentially intimidating feeling to be probed in detail on your past achievements and motivations. To keep you safe this chapter deals with the range of standard questions and offers some suggestions on how to deal with them.

*I keep six honest serving-men
(They taught me all I knew);
Their names are What and Why
and When
And How and Where and Who
(Rudyard Kipling).*

Types of questions:

Interviewers tend to use the following types of questions:

 Open Questions

An open question is one where the answer can vary in length.

Examples:

→ *What attracts you to this job?*

→ *What do you think of...?*

→ *Tell me about yourself?*

HINT: Avoid spinning out your answer!

Probing (or Follow-up) Questions

Questions which follow up on an answer you have just given and look for more information.

Examples:

→ *How did you do that?*

→ *Can you tell me more about the problems you mentioned a moment ago?*

→ *When did the difficulties with X start...?*

Closed Questions

Defined as questions where the answer can be YES or NO or a specific piece of information.

Examples:

→ *Who opened the post?*

→ *How much did it cost to produce?*

→ *On what date did the system go live?*

Hypothetical Questions

Designed to test how you would deal with a specific situation related to the job.

Examples:

→ *How would you give feedback to a difficult member of staff?*

→ *How would you break bad news to a customer?*

HINT: In your answer try to incorporate previous experience: e.g. What I normally do in this situation is to ask lots of questions and reassure the customer... as when confronted with... I...

Panel 4.1

How Interviewers can get it wrong!

When Interviewers ask the wrong type of question!

It may be comforting to know that Interviewers frequently make mistakes. Here are some of the common ones:

❶ Multiple Questions
The Interviewer starts to ask one question which grows into another, and then maybe a third question in the same breath! This shows that the Interviewer is not very skilled. Another form of the multiple question is where two questions are connected by an 'or' statement.

→ *Example: Would you be dealing with the customers or would you be on the computer?*

→ Think carefully about this one – the answer could be a simple yes. It also shows that the Interviewer hasn't prepared properly and is thinking on the fly.

❷ Asking too many closed questions
→ Another frequent fault of Interviewers is their tendency (especially when under pressure) to ask too many closed questions. This gives them selective information about the candidate as they are not really allowing the candidate to explain himself/herself.

❸ Trick questions
→ There are some questions that are traditionally asked which may be incriminating, for example "Tell me, have you ever lied to a client?" These questions are much rarer than they were because Interviewers are now aware of Interviewee rights under equality legislation which requires that interviews be properly structured and run. However, there are occasional breaches of good practice.

❹ 'Good Cop, Bad Cop'
→ Where the questioning switches from one Interviewer to another, with one being 'nice' and the other not so. On some occasions this can be a good and useful tactic, but the problem about this type of routine is that the information collected can be very scattered. Unless the Interviewers are very practiced they may be seriously at cross purposes. From the Interviewer's point

of view it can send out a very negative impression of the company? Would you want to work to a boss who would subject you to the third degree? Not if you had any choice.

Deep probing techniques

Interviewers expect you to answer their questions but in assessing your answers they will be looking for the following:

❶ What's the nature of the data you are giving them: facts, opinions, waffle?

❷ Are you specific on facts, figures, names or dates?

❸ What are you leaving out?

❹ How do the pieces of your answers fit together into a pattern?

❺ Do you construct propositions or arguments that are tight and persuasive or loose and generalised?

❻ What is the context of your information? Is the data you are giving out of proportion to the whole picture?

❼ Do you use generalisations a lot? E.g. Well-motivated staff *always* perform!

❽ Are you using specific names, brands, reputations to try and influence them by association? E.g. Microsoft asked me to do a report!

❾ Are you telling the whole truth? Most people who lie provide information that is mostly true but exploit the fact that they will get the benefit of the doubt.

❿ What's your language — that of feeling, information or strong belief?

⓫ Are you specific about your role in anything you have done?

⓬ How relevant is your answer?

⓭ How do you structure your answer?

⓮ Do you wait before answering?

⓯ Does your pattern of eye contact, voice inflection, gestures change during your answers?

Unsatisfactory answers to any of the above can raise some doubts in Interviewers' minds and may trigger searching probing questions!

How long should an answer be?

The key issues re the length of answers are shown in Panel 4.2 opposite.

Panel 4.2

Length of answers

→ As a guide keep your answers SHORT

→ As a general rule longer answers should last between 30 seconds and a minute unless the matter is particularly complex and you are being questioned by specialists (who will be able to process longer answers). Beyond 30 seconds, information retention is difficult for the listener-particularly if the information is not well structured

→ Give preference to longer answers about areas that are core or critical to the job. You can be a bit more expansive, for example in providing evidence of results you have achieved – if you are being asked about hobbies or interests – keep it short

→ Avoid telling stories with a lot of detail. People tend to lose track of time in storytelling mode!

Panel 4.3

Being alert to Interviewer's signals

→ Check in with the Interviewers non-verbally to see if they are engaging with your answer. Be prepared to wind up your answer if you feel you are losing connection

→ Look for positive signals which can be quite subtle – nods, small noises and smiles indicate that you may be doing well

→ Try to develop an awareness of the Interviewers' changing state of mind – if you have provided a particularly convincing piece of data you may become aware of the Interviewer relaxing and giving you more space.

→ Is the Interviewer's stance similar to your own ('mirroring'). If so, you may be in rapport. Watch for changes

Panel 4.4

Structuring your answers

See information on competency interviewing in the previous chapter. Additional structures you can use would include:

→ EVIDENCE

When making statements, always link them to EVIDENCE-that clearly demonstrates that you know what you are talking about

→ POLAR

- Problem
- Opportunity
- Limits
- Action
- Final Result

→ HYPOTHESIS

Data observed and Conclusion. (Taken from the Scientific Method)

→ GAP ANALYSIS

What you expected versus what you observed – how the difference was explained

Dealing with the 'opinion question'

This is where you are asked to present your thinking on a controversial topic – for example you might be asked to present on the question: *Should we cut staff or services to the public?*

Your fear is that you are being put into a position where you might incriminate yourself. *How do you protect yourself?*

In this situation you should follow the principles of effective persuasion by presenting ideas or information that will be agreeable to all in the initial stages so that you are maximising areas of agreement before areas of controversy. Use these points of agreement to build your argument. Present an alternative point of view and compare the two before declaring your position. If you declare your position at the outset you are more likely to face probing questions in a less than favourable way!

A topic like this is controversial and you might think that neither position is the right one.

What is being tested here is your ability to present both sides of an argument.

> ➔ HINT: Provide the Evidence. If you claim you are a natural, follow up the statement with the evidence.

Panel 4.5

Structure for controversial questions

→ **Step 1:** Decide what your position is — this should be the last idea that you present

→ **Step 2:** Give brief background to the issue

→ **Step 3:** Present the points in favour of whichever proposition your audience is most likely to agree with

→ **Step 4:** Present the opposing position

→ **Step 5:** Contrast and evaluate the points

→ **Step 6:** Present your position ("on balance then...")

This will show your audience that you can think objectively around a controversial issue.

Preparing for the ten standard questions

It is clearly impossible to anticipate all the likely questions you might be asked in an interview. However, there are some common tried and trusted general questions that professional Interviewers tend to fall back on — in addition to the competency questions covered in Chapter 3.

One of the most common mistakes you can make is preparing for the interview as if you were preparing for an exam — by preparing set answers to set questions — and parroting these answers at the interview. This type of preparation may blind you to the fact that the interview is a conversation where particular topics may be probed in more depth than others.

You may have to judge the amount of information you give and be open to the levels of probing that the Interviewer requires. You could spend a lot of time wading through books entitled "Answers to the World's Greatest Interview Questions". What you will get for all this effort will be generic answers to generic questions. Other downsides are that (a) you will waste a lot of time preparing questions that will never be asked, (b) you may make yourself more nervous than before and (c) it will distract from valuable research time.

Here are 10 questions that are asked regularly — together with some strategies for dealing with them. Each of the questions also hides other questions — and I have indicated the 'questions behind the questions'.

❶ Tell Me About Yourself (TMAY)

The question behind the question: Can you be brief in describing yourself in a professional way? Are you the same person I see in your resumé?

This is a standard introductory question. What is needed here is a concise 30 second to one minute introduction about you: current job or role, qualifications, experience, results you can achieve and where you see yourself going in the future.

Example: *"I am Dara O'Keeffe, currently Sales Account Manager with Treston Industries. I graduated with a Business Degree in 2000 and have worked with Treston since then having been promoted twice. I manage over 50 Client Accounts with combined annual turnover of €38m and since I got this job two years ago I have been growing the business by an average of 20% per annum. I am also studying for a part-time MBA with the Open University. I am interested in moving into a senior strategic position in Business Development."* (90 words)

The answer to this question should also relate your experience to the job you are looking for.

The sample answer given above has a structure with the following elements:

→ Name and current role

→ Background: Academic and Professional

→ The results you have achieved in your current job

→ Key areas of expertise and skills

→ Where you can contribute in the future

There are other elements you can consider in your response:

→ Why this organisation or field interests you

→ Current major projects you have in hand

→ Recent successes or awards

→ How you are regarded/viewed in the industry

→ Countries or territories where you operate

If you are planning your own introduction you should consider writing your own personal **WHO's WHO?** entry. Look at a few professional directories to see how other people summarise their careers.

You should also ensure that your brief introduction includes a characteristic statement about yourself that would help the Interviewer remember you.

The TMAY introduction is important because it sets the tone for the rest of the interview.

The following are not useful in your introduction:

→ Generalised, woolly statements about yourself and where you are from!

→ A lack of structure in your opening statement

→ Inappropriate personal disclosure about your weaknesses

→ Boastful statements!

→ Claiming you are an excellent communicator!

Expect to be probed on your prepared answer; a common probe is: "That's about you, professionally − but tell me about you as a person?" What is required here is a summary of how you achieve your results, how you work, your traits and what gives you most satisfaction.

A possible response might go along these lines:

"My managers have described my work as being thorough, and well planned. In teams I am usually assigned the role of chair and I enjoy helping people with different agendas work to a common purpose. However, I am versatile enough to

play other roles according to the requirements of the job in hand and the needs of the people charged to carry it out."

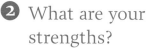

❷ What are your strengths?

The question behind the question: What can you do for me?

What is required here is your own estimate of what your strongest skills are, what are the areas of knowledge you have most developed and how you like to be described. Any information you have from performance reviews which give an indication of how your performance is viewed is very useful here.

Example: *"I have developed my programming skills to level 5 and can diagnose and fix problems in the following business packages........ I have studied German for the last 5 years and can conduct negotiations in that language. As a team leader I have received very positive feedback on dealing with potential conflict in a multi-team environment."*

Strengths can be defined as **key skills.**

To prepare adequately for this question you need to complete a proper skills inventory on yourself

→ What are your best skills? Are they with people, information or things?

→ What skills help you to do your current job properly?

→ What skills or abilities got you through school or college?

→ What do other people ask you to do?

→ What are your most marketable skills?

→ What skills are easier for you than others? (You have a certain knack for...)

→ What skills do you continually fall back on?

→ What are the low level skills? (Everybody has these) – screen these out!

Strengths can also be defined as your areas of **knowledge** – including the following

→ What you studied at school or college

→ On-the-job expertise – including product and customer knowledge

→ Professional contacts and networks

Strengths can also be described as **traits** – how others tend to describe you:

→ Patient

→ Persevering

→ Solution-centred

Avoid woolly self-descriptions such as 'professional', unless you are going to substantiate why you are so

❸ What are your weaknesses?

The question behind the question: How self-aware are you?

One of the most difficult interview questions. What you are being asked here is how aware you are of yourself and your impact on others.

A professional weakness may be considered to include the following:

→ Something that is not a natural strength

→ A problem/weakness that you have overcome

→ A performance issue on which you have been coached successfully

→ An area where you have to work harder than others

→ A task you would prefer not to do or to delegate to somebody else – if you had the choice

→ A weakness is something that has taken you longer to master than others – but which you now can manage

44

→ A weakness is something that you tend to overlook because your eye is on something else

→ A weakness is something that you are constantly working on

Don't let your weaknesses phase you — we **all** have them; others seem to be better at hiding them! You would need to have thought this one through and have several points prepared. What is **not** required is a catalogue of your personal failings or bad habits. Such a list could cost you the interview. What is needed is an honest assessment of areas where you are aware of your lack of facility or talent and how you have recognised and dealt with these.

Some examples:

→ *Because I am naturally outgoing I tend to over-contribute in team discussions. Following feedback from my boss and colleagues I have learned to listen better and read non-verbal signals from colleagues*

→ *I am a recent convert to technology. However, I have learned some core skills from doing an ECDL programme which I funded myself. I can now prepare costing spreadsheets which are used by other members of my team*

→ *Because I prefer to work with the big picture I tend to be less*

effective with fine detail. As a manager, I have learned to delegate such work — and where that is not an option I work in tandem with other colleagues to make sure I don't lose sight of important items

→ *I have learned to keep my irritation to myself when colleagues fail to deliver — I have learned to get delivery using my assertion skills but in a respectful way*

Further probes may ask for something that is a real weakness. Do not fall into the trap of exposing personal flaws or failings.

❹ What differentiates you from anybody else?

The question behind the question: How will we remember you?

Note: the question is **not** what makes you better than anybody else?

Differentiation is about the skills you have that others don't have, the unique experience or project that you were involved in.

Handy differentiators are things like language skills.

e.g. I got my Masters in Brussels so I can respond to Customer Queries in Dutch, German and English.

My managers have remarked that I can remember more names of clients than anybody else on the team. I have no difficulty putting names on the 250 people who pass through our branch on a regular basis. Anybody else can cope with about 100.

Panel 4.6

LIP – Leading Interviewers towards your Preferences

Try this very useful technique:

→ When talking of any topic, just mention in passing a preferred topic that might also be of interest to the Interviewer(s)

→ Do not provide any great detail

→ You will likely get a question on this topic either immediately or soon afterwards

→ By using LIP you can direct the Interviewer(s) into your preferred agenda

→ Do not overuse this technique!

---

❺ Why should we give you the job?

The question behind the question:

What are the four or five things I should say to my Managing Director about you that would convince him/her that you are the right person for the job.

The **Crunch** Question. Possible answers:

Because I have what you are looking for, I understand what the job entails -I can do it (and would be happy doing it for the foreseeable future).

I know all about your company and what it's like to work here and I can see this as a place I can contribute to and grow in.

Be prepared to articulate the four or five points which your claim on the job rests: For example-

→ I have 10 years experience in Sales Training

→ I have consistently produced results above the set targets

→ I have received company and national awards

→ I am very familiar with your company's products and processes

→ I am clear about the

requirements of the job, its future challenges and how I would deal with them.

❻ Why does this job interest you?

The questions behind the question:

What will make you stay with us?
What's in it for you?
What do you really want?
Do we have the same interests?

Consider carefully what is being asked here – your understanding of what the company is best at – and how it matches what you are good at and enjoy doing?

Some examples:

→ *I understand your company is at the leading edge of applying multimedia solutions to internet retailing. As I have both qualifications and experience in this area I am looking for opportunities to contribute to creating solutions in the retailing environment*

→ *Ipson Financial Services is well-known in the marketplace as providing the best in-house training programme for staff who are interested in its specific areas of specialisation – international investment and globalisation. As these are areas I have studied in College I am interested in being part of this work.*

→ *My research brought me to your website and to your Ethical Statement of how you do business in the Third World. Success for me in my career should involve making a return to society in some form or another. Your projects in International Co-Operation would allow me to do that, gain some valuable skills and learn about myself.*

❼ What Salary are you expecting?

The question behind the question:

Can we afford you?
Are you worth it?
Are you aware of your market value?

See Chapter 8 for more on salary negotiation.

❽ Where do you see yourself in five years time?

The questions behind the question:

Do you know where the industry/ company/job is going?
Do you know where you are going and how you might grow in a role like this one?
How open are you to change?
Do you understand our vision, mission and values?

Some Interviewees pull faces or groan when this question is asked.

This type of non-verbal response could cost you the interview. Interviewers like this question (or alternative forms of it) because it tests how well you understand the job, the organisation's culture and how you might fit in. Interviewers may see you in the job and so should you. Try to visualise how you would grow into your new job and manage the changes. Review your last job and how it changed over five years.

Some Examples:

→ *I would like to think I will remain in this industry — and hopefully within your organisation. That however will depend on our on-going contentment with each other*

→ *I hope to be in a job and an organisation that values change, as change and growth are very important to me.*

❾ How would your colleagues describe you?

The questions behind the question:

What are your traits?
How do you perform in a team?
What do your colleagues rely on you for?
How self-aware are you?

The Interviewer wants to know if your understanding of yourself is in line with their observations and any feedback you would have received in the past. See the piece on traits in Question 2 above. *This could also be seen as an elegant variation on the question:*
What are your weaknesses?
— see Question 3 above.

❿ Is there anything else you would like to add?

The questions behind the question:

Are you well-briefed on this interview?
Have you been in control of your part of the interview?
Have you made all the points we need to hear from you?

In communication we are influenced by the phenomenon of **primacy** and **recency**

→ PRIMACY
Being more influenced by first impressions

→ RECENCY
Being more influenced by impressions made on parting.

This means the final impression you leave with the Interviewers has to be positive and has to show that you have been in proper control of your end of the interview.

Before you answer this question you should pause to consider the situation and observe your Interviewers: Are they under time pressure? If they are you have just a few seconds to respond.

Here are your major options:

→ Take a few seconds to reflect and, if you cannot think of anything, thank the board positively for their time and hand back to them

→ If anything occurs to you that you think will make a major impact on the decision, present it clearly and concisely in a few short sentences

→ Briefly present any additional piece of information or benefit of your experience which would help the board make their decision

→ Re-emphasise briefly why your experience and knowledge would help the company in the results you could achieve for them

→ State what attracted you to the company — their reputation, their image in the marketplace and state that you would be very happy working in such a place

→ Quote something from the company's mission and values that relates to the way that you work or have delivered results in the past

→ State that the interview has been an interesting and valuable developmental opportunity for you

Avoid the following:

→ Asking when you will hear the decision (unless there is a real need to do so)

→ Making boastful statements about yourself

→ Making disparaging comments about other Interviewees ("I think you will find that nobody else has my experience.")

→ Veiled threats ("You do not know what you are missing if you do not give me the job")

→ Showing clear relief that the interview is over (at last!). *The Interviewers will remember the clear relief on your face and perhaps question your ability to handle stress!*

Your last non-verbal exchange with the board should be positive with good eye contact. Imagine you had just met your new work colleagues — who were about to welcome you to the organisation.

In this chapter we have treated:

→ All of the main types of questions with which you will be confronted, and

ACTIVITY:
Your personal answers to the 10 Great Questions

See exercise 9 within the Workbook Supplement at the end of the book.

➲ Take time out to list your answers to the 10 standard interview questions. It will help you refine your thinking before the interview.

→ Optimum responses that you can use

In our next chapter we will briefly look at presentations, which are now more common in selection.

Summary of Chapter 4

→ Understand the question behind the question

→ Take time to think before you answer

→ Be clear about your strengths, skills and knowledge gaps and how you have dealt with them

→ Practice your responses to the usual expected questions

→ Keep answers brief

→ Be sure to provide EVIDENCE with your statements

→ Use LIP- Leading Interviewers towards your Preferences

→ Conclude the interview positively

→ Interviewers use a wide variety of questions — focus on the question. Be clear exactly what is being looked for

→ Interviewers can get it wrong. Interviewing may be very structured but is not an exact science!

Presentations and preparing for them

5

Chapter outline
Presentations and preparing for them

→ Preparing and structuring your
   presentation: the three steps
→ Grooming and Presentation: Dress Code

Introduction

Many selection procedures, particularly those for senior appointments, now require candidates to make formal presentations.

Survey after survey has shown that for many people fear of giving presentations ranks above all other fears. Even for the experienced presenter any presentation, no matter how short, is something you don't just walk into cold.

In selection situations you may be asked to make a presentation on such topics as:

→ A generic current issue relevant to the job or industry: *e.g. should all public transport be privatised?* The issue may be deliberately controversial

→ Your vision of how you would meet the challenges of the job

→ An evaluation of a product or service offered by the organisation

→ Your case for getting the job

→ The longer term strategic view that the organisation should adopt

Usually such presentations are judged very strictly on time. Powerpoint may or may not be used. Many presentations do not require aids. Occasionally, participants are asked to use only a flipchart.

So what are the steps in preparing an excellent presentation?

➋ 1 – Prepare Your Material

➋ 2 – Prepare Yourself

➋ 3 – Prepare for your audience

➊ Prepare Your Material

Establish your objective:

→ What is the aim of your talk – to persuade, inform or to entertain?

→ What should your audience, know, think or feel at the end of your presentation?

→ What would be the appropriate follow-up to your talk?

Who is your audience?

→ What positions do they hold? What influence do they have? What will influence them?

→ What do they know about you and your subject – what do they need to know? Is there anybody in particular in your audience who you need to influence – or who can help you?

→ How will you involve them in your presentation?

What are the main points you have to get across?

List, or better still, brainstorm your main content headings, even better still brainstorm your points, list them, return to them later and brainstorm again.

How will you structure the presentation?

Consider at an early stage the structure for the presentation and ensure that you see clearly the BEGINNING, MIDDLE and END of the presentation.

Instant Presentation

On occasions one may be asked to make a presentation on the spur of the moment. When this occurs SCRAP may help.

S Explain the SITUATION

C Outline the COMPLEXITIES

R Give options as to how problems can be RESOLVED

A Recommend a Course of ACTION

P Present the IMPLEMENTATION Plan

→ Situation phase: Keep it brief – just a few details to give the background. Present basic information concisely

→ Complexities phase: Describe the Problem or Difficulty – this is where you present conflicting or contrasting ideas. The basic information may be ambiguous and you have to deal with this

→ Resolution: This is where you articulate possible options for action. Keep the one you

---

Panel 5.1

What Audiences Remember:

→ First Impressions

→ Information specific to their needs

→ New or striking points of information

→ A good simple clearly presented structure

→ Your parting remarks – how you ended (the recency effect)

want them to go for till last (remember the recency or proximity effect)

→ Action Phase: Where you articulate the action or position you are advocating

→ Implementation Planning: This is where you articulate the first steps in the implementation of your solutions or suggestions.

Make sure you conclude the presentation strongly. It is useful to link back to your opening and remind your audience of your objective.

Two other popular generic structures are the **SWOT** and **FORCE FIELD** approaches

SWOT:

STRENGTHS
WEAKNESSES
OPPORTUNITIES and
THREATS

FORCE FIELD: List factors
that work for progress and
contrast them with those that
work against. At the end do a
comparative evaluation and a
judgment as to which is the most
likely to win out over time.

❷ Prepare Yourself

Building Confidence

Confidence is built by good
research and preparation, practice,
arriving on time and preparing
the place where the presentation
is going to take place. Be rested,
dress comfortably and well – use
colours that suit you and make
you feel good – it's your space so
make the best of it!

Panel 5.2

"Make a presentation about the job..."

In the situation where you
are given minimal instruction
as to what is required for
such a presentation about
the job for which you are
being interviewed, you should
consider the following topics:

❶ What you think the
challenges of the job
might be

❷ Challenges facing the
organisation that will be
reflected in the job

❸ How the job reflects the
strategy, culture and
values of the organisation
(which you have, of course,
researched!)

❹ What is happening in the
organisation's environment
and how it would affect
performance on the job.
(The economy is on an
upswing, therefore the
market is ready for new
products and services –
you see the role as
encouraging innovation
and development)

❺ How the job matches your
experience, abilities and
traits. "This job requires X,Y
and Z. I have experience in
these because ...." Start with
the job and end with you!

Panel 5.3

VISUALS AIDS: Are best to

→ heighten impact	**Avoid the following:**
→ illustrate complex material	→ Too many visual aids (eg. too many Powerpoint slides)
→ summarise information	
→ flag sections of your presentation	→ Unclear layout
	→ Bad lettering
→ provide a change of mood or pace	→ Certain colours (Red, Orange and Yellow are problematical)
Audiovisual aids are just that — aids to better presentation. They have to be managed and not allowed to dominate the presentation.	→ Inappropriate use of the aids (see following section)
	→ Aids not in place at the right time, nor rehearsed.

What about nerves?

Everybody has them but remember they don't look as bad from the outside as they feel from the inside. If something goes wrong your audience don't usually notice immediately so you have time to fix things. Don't tell them you've made a mistake unless you have to. Don't put yourself down if something goes wrong. *One word of caution: if you have skimped on your preparation — it will catch up on you when you start the presentation.*

❸ Prepare for your audience

When approaching any presentation your must try as best as possible to understand your audience and where they are coming from. You will need to assess the amount of knowledge they have on the subject of the presentation and therefore must pitch it at a level with which they can equate. In interview situations you do not know too much about the audience except that they are going to pass judgment on the quality of your presentation vis-a-vis your overall application. You need to bear this very much in mind when preparing for the presentation and ensure that you relate it as far as possible directly to their need.

Visual aids can be used as an aid to getting your message across but not as the principal medium of your message. You yourself in interview presentations in particular should allow the message come from you personally in such a way that you can relate in posture and visual contact directly to your interview panel.

Panel 5.4

HINTS on USING LAPTOPS:

→ Make sure the laptop is plugged in and not operating off batteries. You could get a shock if it runs out power during your presentation. Know your computer settings.

→ Rehearse the sequence of booting up your PC and switching on the projector. Beware of both items going into standby mode!

→ Keep the presentation simple, do not crowd slides.

→ Use as few slides as possible.

FLIPCHART:

Good For:

→ Mapping your structure

→ Highlighting key points

→ Summaries and simple graphics

→ Self-pacing (you can write your cues on them in light pencil and your audience won't see anything)

→ Building up a display.

Remember the visual aids are just that — an aid; you are the real medium of communication.

Grooming and Presentation: Dress Code

Research the dress code of the organisation — if in doubt err on the conservative side. The general rule is dress for confidence, comfort and positive impact. Dress to show you are taking the interview seriously, and dress conservatively and in a business-like style to be on the safe side while allowing just enough room to express a little of your personality.

⮕ For men:

→ Preference should be given to blue, grey or black for suits

→ Shirts should be in plain colours and textures — ties to match. Check collar size, you can become very constricted and nervous if the size is too small

→ Get advice if you think you have skin problems — presentation is an issue! Dandruff or eczema are not fatal diseases but can be in an interview because it may raise doubt as to how you will look to clients and colleagues!

● For Women:

As above, dress for both positive impact and comfort.

The general tone of your dress should be business-like. A business suit with either trousers or skirt with a blouse is best. A day dress and jacket is also acceptable. Skirt length and necklines should be modest. You can afford to have a little more colour in the outfit, particularly with the blouse or shirt, but nothing too garish or too patterned.

Wear stockings or tights and avoid using fake tan. Normal rules of good grooming apply — i.e. tidy hair and neat nails. If you wear your hair in a fringe, have it trimmed so it is not in you eyes and tie your hair back if you can, so you reveal as much of your face as possible. A little jewellery is fine, but avoid noisy bangles

and dangling ear rings — jewelry should complement your outfit but not distract. Your handbag should be a neat size and not stuffed too full — a big bulky bag may give an impression of being a bit disorganised.

If you wish to wear make-up, err on the side of too little rather than too much, especially when it comes to lipstick, which should use a neutral colour.

If in doubt err on the conservative side — minimize risks of nerves because you feel the image you are presenting is not quite right!

ACTIVITY:
Presentation Preparation

See Exercise 10 within the Workbook Supplement at the end of the book.

● Take time out to prepare yourself for presentations. Even if you don't know the subject of your presentation it is extremely useful to have practiced a few and have some generic structures ready.

Summary of Chapter 5

→ Prepare, prepare, prepare

→ Prepare your material

→ Prepare yourself

→ Prepare for your audience

→ Use generic structures such as SWOT or SCRAP — be practiced in their use

→ Keep slides simple

→ Keep everything simple

→ Test your laptop.

→ Pay attention to grooming and presentation.

A more detailed treatment of Presentations can be found in another book within this series

Impactful Presentations — *Best Practice Skills*
By Yvonne Farrell

www.ManagementBriefs.com

Rehearsals and Last-Minute Preparation

Chapter outline
Rehearsals and Last-Minute Preparation

→ Interview coaching
→ Chase pre-interview nerves:
    use visualisation
→ Simulating the interview:
    pre-interview rehearsal techniques
→ Using Video
→ Waiting for the interview

Introduction

As part of the in-depth preparation for the interview, the most effective thing you can do is to prepare for the interview in a number of different ways apart from reading up about the company or the job. The more ways you prepare the better. Try to anchor what you have to say in your interview so that you will be less likely to 'dry' on the day itself.

In pre-interview situations it is very beneficial to get yourself some coaching from friends and colleagues. You can do this through the various initiatives that we outline on Panel 6.1 overleaf.

Panel 6.1

Pre-Interview Coaching Tips

❶ Read the job description and your application to be familiar with areas of overlap — anticipate gaps. List the twenty questions (or so) you expect to be asked; prepare your answers in bullet form. See if you can fit it onto one page. Get a friend to coach you on the answers to your twenty questions. Instruct them to signal you once you have spoken for one minute. Ask them to check against the bulleted answers

❷ Talk over with someone your thoughts about the job — the challenges you expect and how you might deal with them

❸ Ask trusted colleagues and mentors for feedback

❹ Review your performance reviews to build up information on your strengths and areas for development — discuss them with a mentor, boss or support person

❺ Ask a friend to help you review your last five years at work and outside it. Ask them to question you on your five year plan for the future — focus on how you expect your life inside and outside work to develop (e.g. as children grow up and your industry or field adjust to an ever-changing future)

❻ Ask several friends to frame challenging interview questions — get them to imagine themselves as members of your interview board

Chase the pre-interview nerves: Use positive visualisation

Many people perform badly at interviews because they put their energies into visualising failure and spend their energies worrying about the terrible things that might happen. When they get into the actual interview they realise that they have nothing prepared and nothing to fall back on. You can use positive visualisation to imagine the interview before it happens as shown in Panel 6.2 opposite.

Simulating the interview: pre-interview rehearsal techniques

Using Video

Reviewing video of question and answer exchanges provides powerful, positive and reassuring feedback for both Interviewers and Interviewees. Thus you could benefit from using a camcorder to practice your interview; it can show you information you can't get easily any other way such as:

→ How clear your voice is and how far it carries

Panel 6.2

5 Positive Visualisation scenarios

1 How would it feel if I had just done the perfect interview? How would I feel?

Hold that thought for a few moments — it proves that you have some control over your mental state!

2 How would it feel if I were asked exactly the right questions that I had prepared and I could visualise the Interviewers listening intently and positively to my answers.

Unrealistic maybe, but more pleasant than constantly visualising your Interviewers trying to catch you out.

3 What would it be like if I did dry up and I had several alternatives to deal with the nerves?

You can have this luxury if you prepare for it.

4 Imagine the interview has just finished and you have just left the room; what would you like the Interviewers to say about you?

This technique can help you to focus on the four or five key messages you would like to leave with your Interviewers.

5 Think of a successful interview in the past- maybe the one where you got your first job. How did you feel when you got notice of your success?

Past positive feelings can be powerful motivators for the future.

→ Your eye contact (or lack of it) and how it changes

→ Showing your rapport patterns

→ General impression and impact

→ It is often very helpful to use the camcorder a number of times — so that you get used to seeing your self in action. Be sure to use the camcorder to build, not destroy, your confidence

→ You should take the opportunity to ask someone else to ask you the questions; when you playback you should time how long your answers are — you are likely to be very surprised

You may feel very self-conscious when you start using it first. Persist, as the video is one of the best ways of gauging your impact.

Panel 6.3

Matts's experience with the video:

"It was weird watching myself on video — I spoke much faster than I thought I did —and I dropped my words at the end of the sentences. But the thing that shocked me was that I kept interrupting the end of the Interviewer's questions with the start of my answers!"

The most common mistake with video is using it to show your weakness as an Interviewee. It should be used to check back to see your progress. Gentle persistence is the key! Your objective in using video should be to find the places where you are communicating well and to use those as your benchmarks. Your objective should be to build your communication style — not to recreate yourself. Don't be afraid to experiment — you won't have that luxury in the interview itself!

Using a mirror

Some people find this helpful but it might be worth considering the following:

→ Mirrors don't talk back!

→ Mirrors show your image the wrong way around!

Waiting for the interview

When you get to the interview, be sure to arrive in good time — allow for everything — including parking time. Better to arrive half an hour early than one minute late!

→ In the real world few interview boards runs exactly to time — they start late, more often than not. So be prepared for about 15 minutes delay before you are brought into the interview room

→ Use the time just to breathe and relax. The act of breathing releases chemicals into your bloodstream that will reduce your stress

→ Sit comfortably and ground yourself.

Do not cram your preparation into the last few hours/minutes before the interview. Finish all preparation 24 hours before the interview if you can. It will give your subconscious brain time to process all the information you have fed into it.

ACTIVITY:
Last Minute Changes

See the Workbook Supplement at the end of the book.

➔ Take time out to attend to the last-minute details. Leave yourself time to relax just before the interview.

Summary of Chapter 6

→ Use friends or trusted associates to coach you on your interview technique

→ Visualise your interview in a number of different ways — be positive but realistic

→ Use video in a positive way — find what works in your communication style and build on it

→ Pace yourself coming up to the interview — leave yourself plenty of time to think

→ Arrive in time and be prepared to wait.

7

Communication and Rapport during the Interview

Chapter outline
Communication and Rapport during the Interview

→ Verbal and non-verbal communication
→ Active Listening
→ Matching rapport patterns
→ Dealing with Nerves during the Interview
→ Interviewers get nervous too!
→ Disasters, including 'drying'

Introduction

Establishing rapport is critical. Do all in your power to 'connect' with the Interviewer(s)

One of your main tasks is to establish positive verbal and non-verbal contact with the Interviewer. If you are in good contact with the Interviewer both of you will have better control

Verbal and non-verbal communication

It is frequently claimed that up to 85% of communication at interviews is non-verbal — Interviewers pay more attention to the way you communicate than what you are trying to communicate. The reality is that the balance in emphasis shifts from time to time. If you are establishing rapport or having a nervous episode the Interviewer's attention may be predominantly on your body language. If you are in close rapport with the Interviewer they may be more focussed on what you are saying. It is also important to remember that in situations of panel interviews rapport has to be established with more than one person, the requirement may be to swing back and forth from one person to another.

Communication from the Interviewer's view point works in the three dimensions:

→ Content — what is being said/discussed

→ What the Interviewer sees

→ What the Interviewer hears

A practical result of this is that what you are saying may be coloured by the way that you are saying it! Another practical result is that we pick up signals from eye contact (or lack of it), from tone of voice and from stance/seating posture quicker that we hear and interpret the words being used. It takes the brain time to interpret the words but body language can be picked up instantly.

If you are hesitant and lack confidence in your body language your message may lose credibility dramatically.

Active Listening

This form of listening is called 'active listening' because the Interviewer is listening in several ways at once.

Interviewers are trained in *active listening* to behave as shown in Panel 7.1 overleaf.

Panel 7.1

Interviewer active listening behaviours

Professional Interviewers are trained to:

→ Suspend judgment as long as possible

→ Hear detailed information

→ Detect gaps

→ Check how arguments are built logically

→ Be sensitive to the emotion behind language

→ Observe patterns in verbal and non-verbal behaviour

→ Summarise or repeat what they have heard

→ Support the speaker verbally and non-verbally

Put another way, the components of active listening that Interviewers try to use are:

→ I understand what you are saying

→ I understand the thinking behind what you say

→ I am trying to 'get the big picture'

→ I suspend judgment

→ I am actively supporting you the speaker

This makes listening a complex and exhausting one for the Interviewer. You can help by keeping your answers short and well-structured and taking your time to listen actively and fully to the Interviewer.

FACT

One of the most frequent mistakes made by Interviewees is not listening properly to the question being asked and therefore answering the wrong question. Take your time and detach yourself from your thoughts about how you are doing and just listen to the question!

Matching rapport patterns

It is useful to know if you are doing well in the interview. Look for the following:

1 Interviewer engaging in good eye contact.

2 Nods

3 Encouraging sounds

4 Interviewer moves slightly closer

5 The Interviewer unconsciously matches your non-verbal behaviour.

This form of rapport is called 'matching' and is a sign that you and the Interviewer are communicating as equals and that you may be doing well.

Warning signs that things may not be going well are:

1 The Interviewer draws back

2 You lose eye contact

3 There is a sharp intake of breath!

Because patterns of eye contact vary between different cultures and nationalities it is impossible to generalise. However, observing patterns of non-verbal behaviour is useful.

Dealing with Nerves during the interview

Why nerves are essential to the process in *seven words*:

No nerves = no positive stress = no performance

As simple as that – No nerves, no awareness, no performance.

Nerves keep you alert and focussed. If you have prepared properly you will still be nervous but will be able to perform – it may not be the most comfortable experience in the world.

"There are two types of nerves. The first type is when you go out to play a concert and you have practiced all you can – and you're still nervous. The second type is where you go out play the concert knowing you haven't practiced enough. I much prefer the first type of nerves."

Arthur Rubenstein,
Pianist.

The main reason people get nervous at interviews is because they have not prepared properly or in sufficient time. You walk into the interview and say something and your brain registers the thought 'this is not quite right' – and then you get really nervous.

The Amnesia Factor

Interviews happen at warp speed or in slow motion!

Interviewers and Interviewees have one common problem — both are very poor at recalling the detail of what happened during the interview. Research also shows that different Interviewers may differ in their interpretation of the data before them.

Warp Speed Interviewing?

"Next thing it was lunchtime."

This is where the Interviewer wonders where the last two hours went.

The Interviewee can recall the start of the interview and the end — but what happened in the middle?

Slow motion Interviews?

"The seconds seem like minutes, the minutes seem like hours."

The Interviewee makes a mistake, or gets stuck and imagines the passing of seconds as if they were hours and stays stuck in the belief that the interview is now lost — and the rest is suffering. At the same moment the Interviewer may be having a very different perception ("they are taking their time — good!")

Why do these two things happen?

→ Interviewer or Interviewee are not focussing on the matter in the present moment — being stuck at some point in the past or the future

→ Our tendency to connect pieces of information together in judgments — wanting to move forward

Interviewers and Interviewees have one common problem — both are very poor at recalling the detail of what happened during the interview.

→ Preconceptions about what is happening, or should be happening.

When giving 'evidence' within your answers, try to pick incidents that will re-ignite interest among the Interviewer(s).

So, if you feel that your Interviewer is losing concentration you should take this as a signal. You would be wise to focus on some of the remedies outlined in Panel 7.3

Panel 7.3

Remedies for Interviewer concentration loss

Re-establish good rapport with the Interviewer by:

→ Staying in the present moment – be aware of how long your answers are taking

→ Taking things slowly, take time to think

→ Being aware that the Interviewer's concentration may dip

→ Trying to put energy into your answers

Interviewers get nervous too!

It should be reassuring to know that Interviewers get nervous for a number of reasons

→ They are under stress to perform and select the right candidate

→ If it is a promotion they may be interviewing colleagues they know well and may be worried about their subsequent relationships with those colleagues who are not successful

→ There may be tensions between members of the interview board

→ They may not have had time to prepare, or they have limited experience of interviewing.

Interviewers are trained to establish and maintain rapport. Do not be afraid to engage in positive eye contact and rapport. If you are nervous and have good rapport the Interviewer is more likely to help than if you are nervous and disconnected. Another important aspect of rapport and nerves is that when rapport is well established Interviewer and Interviewee mirror each others' behaviour – so if you get nervous, chances are that you are making the Interviewer nervous as well. It is part of your job to support the Interviewer and make them less nervous – which is why you should give them good positive eye contact – and mentally wish them well!

Disasters including 'drying'

Everybody makes mistakes during the interview!

People do not communicate word perfectly – we talk and make small errors all the time – but in the process of being listened to our mistakes are usually ignored in favour of the main message. So if you make a small mistake it may not even be noticed! If you have a good connection with the Interviewer small errors will hardly register.

If you make a noticeable mistake — take time and correct yourself. To help the Interviewer — backtrack slightly in your answer and say what you wanted to say. This can work very much in your favour as it demonstrates to the Interviewer that you are in good control and are properly aware of what you are saying.

Some remedies for 'drying' are listed in Panel 7.4 below:

Panel 7.4

Remedies for 'Drying'

When you totally lose concentration and go blank you have a number of choices as follows:

❶ Take your time! Breathe and focus on the Interviewer. The act of stopping and breathing may relax you and you may recover your answer

❷ If this doesn't work — tell the Interviewer you would like to hear the question again as you have lost track

❸ If you can, backtrack in the answer and try to recover

❹ Tell the Interviewer that you cannot recall the information at this precise moment but you would like to come back to the question at the end of the interview. This is helpful because it shows the Interviewer that you are not trying to avoid the question

❺ Take time to re-orient your chair and your stance relative to the Interviewer. This may buy you time. The act of repositioning yourself may stimulate your creative (right) brain which deals also with space and position and also handles intuitive responses. There is strong anecdotal evidence to show that this strategy is effective

Summary of Chapter 7

→ Listen, listen, listen to the question

→ Everybody gets nervous at interviews — use suggested techniques to minimise nervousness

→ It is possible to be nervous and perform well at the same time

→ Prepare positively in a number of different ways

→ Interviewers get nervous too

→ If you lose track or make a mistake then there are many options for recovery

Salary Negotiation

Chapter outline
Salary Negotiation

→   When to discuss salary
→   Basic Negotiation techniques and
     Salary Negotiation
→   Behaviours of effective negotiators

Introduction

You may have done a very good interview in terms of answering questions as asked. However, people who hire staff are usually under instruction to get the best staff at the right price. Your objective is not to screen yourself out of the final selection process by being unrealistic about your value. To be successful you need to have a sense of what your value is in the marketplace.

When to discuss salary

The general answer to this question is — as late in the interview as possible. Preferably when you are sure that you are a serious candidate, which is probably not until short-list stage.

A job interview is a particular type of sale and as such you should follow the principle of closing any sale: Don't close the interview until you are sure that you are getting buying signals.

Here are some you should look for:

→ When the Interviewer shifts from discussing the job requirements to talking about the benefits of the job

→ A shift in questioning technique from *"what did you do when..."* to *"what would you do if...."*

→ The Interviewer starts asking a lot of questions about you and what you would need

→ Non-verbal signals such as talking faster, change of tone of voice, gesticulating or shifting position to move closer could imply strong interest

→ The HR person comes into play and you notice other members of the interview panel disengaging!

It is inappropriate and inadvisable to discuss salary at the start of any interview.

Candidates who leave the salary negotiation until later in the interview do better than others!

Interviewers ask about salary for a number of reasons:

1 To screen you out of the selection process

2 To identify and possibly rank a final shortlist

3 To gather information about the marketplace

Basic Negotiation techniques and Salary Negotiation

Effective negotiation techniques would require a full book. Briefly, there are four basic stages in the negotiation process and if you hold to these you will get a better result.

❶ Opening Stage

Both parties state their opening positions and agree rules of engagement – i.e. how the discussion is to proceed.

❷ The Exploratory Stage

Both parties explore the other's positions by questioning and clarification. ***Do not discuss any offers until you are clear that you understand the other party's position as well as you do your own.*** Use silence, probing questioning and summaries (as in Chapter 4).

Once there is mutual clarity on positions the Interviewer may put pressure on you by stating that a decision has to made quickly or that the offer expires once you walk out of the door.

❸ The Consolidation Stage

The exploration phase moves from the clarification stage to consolidation stage when "what if ...?" and "If then ...?" type questions are asked.

→ What if... questions:
These questions explore the consequences of hypothetical positions and can be useful in breaking deadlocks.

Here are some sample 'what if...' questions:

What if we reviewed the salary in 6 months?

What happens if I exceed my performance targets?

What would you think if I worked for four days?

What would the package look like if I were to work on partial commission?

→ If... then... questions:
These questions are not actual offers or new positions but harbingers of them. When the language moves from "What if..?" to "If ... then..." amended offers may be put on the table. If this happens, take your time. Silence is your most effective weapon! If you take time to think there may be an additional part to the offer.

Here are some examples of "If... then... "

Would you complete the degree if we paid the fees?

If you give me a commercial mileage rate I can use my car on company business

If you give me access to the profit sharing scheme I would accept the basic salary

If you reduced the probation period I would be happy to accept the package.

This phase emerges when the parties concentrate on convergent rather than divergent issues, thus minimising conflict between them. They try to avoid contentious issues, acting on the assumption that everyone around the negotiation table is anxious to move towards a final settlement.

4 The Decision-Making Stage

If the process has proceeded to amended offer stage further clarification may be needed – keep asking questions! Concessions may be asked for at this stage – look for concessions from the other side first. There is a general principle in negotiation that the first person to concede loses most. Take your time to be clear on what is being offered (and what is not being offered!).

Being asked for your current salary: An inappropriate answer to this question can terminate the interview prematurely! Being asked for your expected salary early on in the interview suggests that the answer may be used to screen you out of the process.

If offered a salary which is below your expectations here are some questions you can ask:

➲ Is this a basic salary?

➲ What are the bonus arrangements?

➲ When is this salary reviewed?

➲ How are salaries linked to performance in the job?

➲ What are the profit or share options?

➲ Are there any staff discount schemes?

➲ Can you describe the pension plan – briefly?

➲ What are the fringe benefits – specifically study loans?

➲ What are your overtime arrangements?

➲ Can one take time off in lieu?

Behaviours of successful negotiators:

The principles that apply in business negotiation are equally true here:

→ Have your research done in advance. The internet is a powerful resource for salary research

→ Don't take a stand early on in the proceedings

→ The best negotiators ask plenty of questions and establish a good rapport with the other party

→ Take your time in answering questions. Use silence strategically

→ If asked "are you ready to discuss salary" remember that, if opportune, you can say no until you have all the information you need

→ Find out all the elements of the salary and benefits package being offered. Make sure you are comparing like with like!

→ Silence is your most effective weapon — take time to think

→ The process is over when numbers are finalised

Summary of Chapter 8

→ Do not discuss salary until you are sure that all other parts of the interview are in place

→ Do your research — know what the industry norms are

→ Ask plenty of questions, summarise — not all parts of the package may be on the table at the start

→ Be aware of the stages of negotiation: move from "What if?" to "If... then" only when you are sure you have all the information you need

→ Your most effective weapon may be to use silence, as appropriate

Reviewing
the Interview

Chapter outline
Reviewing the Interview

→ You did not get the job: *What happened?*
→ Reviewing the interview
→ Checking back on prepared material
→ Asking for and receiving feedback
→ Differentiating between good and
   poor feedback
→ Planning your next interview

Introduction

If you get bad news — which is likely for most interview candidates, especially when you consider the numbers — you will need to do an honest review of what happened. The way you engage with this painful process will determine your future success. Even if you were the most suitable and best-prepared candidate in the world you may not get the job and it is worth considering this so that your future interviews will not be affected by this. The challenge is to understand, to the best of your ability, what actually happened and then build on that for the future — that is the most uncomfortable and the most productive thing you could do.

You did not get the interview: What happened?

There are two possibilities here: (1) You did the best you could and you are mystified about what happened *and* (2) You did not do as well as you expected and you know it.

1 You did the best you could — what happened, what went wrong?

If you did not get the job as expected the following may have happened:

→ You were in the top three or four slot — but they got someone who performed just as well, but at a lower salary

→ You matched all the requirements, but another candidate brought something extra to the table

→ Another candidate was a better fit for the job in terms of image, method of communication or other criteria. *Fit for the job is one of the most critical factors in recruitment and selection*

→ You were too similar to what they had already and they felt they wanted something different

→ In some industries, especially in the technology sector, like

tends to recruit like; this is a particularly dangerous form of bias.

2 You did not do as well as you expected — what happened, what went wrong?

Although there could be many others, here are the main possibilities to consider:

→ You did not do enough preparation

→ You over-prepared — you were preoccupied and stressed and did not listen to the Interviewer's properly

→ You were nervous and remained so during the interview, despite the Interviewer's best efforts

→ Your examples and data were not at the right level

→ You were strong is some areas and weaker in others and the Interviewers were aware of the contrast

→ You did not listen properly to the questions and your answers were not what was actually required

→ Your answers were too long

→ You launched into long, rambling stories and ignored signals from the Interviewers that brevity was required

→ There was little rapport between you and the Interviewers

→ Your documentation was difficult to read and to relate to the job description and the Interviewers could not easily reconcile them

→ You treated the interview as a meaningless ritual — and this was obvious to the Interviewers

Dealing with rejection after interviews:

Remember the maxim:
There is no failure only failure to learn.

Fail, learn, fail better, try again, learn more and succeed.

We all fail but more people are willing to broadcast their successes than their failures. There are many hidden failures out there!

Reviewing the interview

As soon as you can face up to it, review the interview — this may be a painful experience.

Recall and write up what you can remember of the interview. Instead of listing what went wrong

try initially to recall what worked, what answers you were happy with.

Your objective is to rebuild your confidence so that you can perform from a place of confidence in the future.

Identify

→ What worked — what answers went to plan?

→ Where did you get validation from the Interviewers?

→ What did not work?

→ What surprised you?

ACTIVITY:
Last Minute Changes

See Exercise 12 within the Workbook Supplement at the end of the book.

When things go wrong:

If you feel that the interview or competition has been improperly conducted you may consider that you have grounds for complaint. Before you lodge a complaint you should consider taking professional and not necessarily legal advice; find a HR professional who can advise. There are often situations where further action may not be appropriate because of lack of evidence — in reality most potential complaints do not proceed beyond this stage.

The most frequent grounds for complaint are:

→ The successful candidate was less qualified than others

→ The interview was incompetently conducted

As a general rule national law in most countries requires candidates to be treated consistently and fairly and the interview criteria have to be directly related to the job.

→ Discriminatory questioning breaching of equality law e.g. marital status, ethnic or gender issues

→ The Interviewers used different criteria to that given in notices or advertisements

→ Different standards of questioning and evidence asked of different candidates

→ Gender balance on interview panels

→ Inessential criteria used as a indirect way of screening out some candidates — e.g. asking for long and unbroken periods of service which would discriminate against people who had taken maternity leave or career breaks.

As a general rule national law in most countries requires candidates to be treated consistently and fairly and the interview criteria have to be directly related to the job.

If you feel that these principles have been violated you may have grounds for complaint — but check with a professional adviser before you make any approach to the organisation.

Checking back on prepared material

It is useful to check back on the documentation that you used during the interview to ensure that although it was correct, that all the right connections were made with it, by :

→ Checking your documentation and relating it to your memory of the interview

→ Asking yourself if there appeared to be problems with the documentation during the interview?

→ Can you recall the Interviewers having difficulty finding the information they wanted?

Differentiating between good and poor feedback

Giving good feedback is a rare skill. The feedback you get may be poorly delivered.

Bad feedback	Good feedback
① Frequently starts with a negative judgment e.g. *You were weak and unprofessional and you did your career prospects no good either. What were you thinking of? etc.*	① Starts with a clear and positive statement about the process of giving feedback e.g. *I would like to give you feedback to help you for your next application because you gave us clear evidence of your leadership abilities, however the examples were too low level*
② Is woolly and judgmental: e.g *This was not your best, you were weaker than the others*	② Is specific and non-judgmental; e.g. *You provided evidence to us that you had managed the project well and supplied the figures to prove it*
③ Lacks clear examples e.g. You had some woolly answers	③ Gives clear examples and concise observations about what happened. Has the ring of truth e.g. see above
④ Makes you feel bad and saps your confidence	④ Is respectful and gives you hope for the future
⑤ Feedback is one-way; there is no discussion	⑤ Allows you to probe and ask for further information
⑥ Leaves you unclear about what to do in the future	⑥ Gives you suggestions that you know will get results!

Asking for and receiving feedback

If feedback is offered after the interview take the opportunity.

However, remember the following:

→ Your Interviewers may give you limited feedback

→ The feedback may not be expertly or diplomatically given.

Research shows that Interviewers may have difficulty in remembering what happened at interview. Consider that you only had one interview to remember but your Interviewer may have had dozens. Also most interviews are not recorded in transcript form so that almost certainly there will not be a complete record of what happened. Interviewers usually only record their conclusions and the relevant evidence.

If feedback is not forthcoming ask for it on the basis that you want to improve your performance. Resist the temptation to express negative views about the process. Be open to the fact that most people find **giving** feedback an extremely difficult exercise — try and help them as much as possible by being positive, constructive and open. Do not expect too much!

Dealing with promotion feedback

Providing feedback on internal promotion interviews is often difficult, mainly due to the colleague/colleague relationship.

Be alert to these sensitivities and accept fully that your colleague may be quite uncomfortable giving feedback.

Listen well, clarify and be gracious.

e.g. *Thank you very much for the pointers on presenting the financial information. I realised it wasn't going the way I planned. I look forward to using the structure you suggested and will try it in other presentations in the meantime.*

Planning for your next interview:

When you have finished your review and feedback, the following actions are strongly recommended:

❶ Write up your feedback

❷ Amend your CV and other documentation

❸ Consider working with a coach or mentor on some of the suggestions

❹ Decide if you can practice some of the suggestions given to you in other situations.

Summary of Chapter 9

→ You may have been in the final shortlist and not know it!

→ Take time to establish what worked for you at the interview instead of dwelling on failure and becoming discouraged or paralysed as a result

→ There is no failure — only failure to learn

→ If you feel your interview was incorrectly conducted get proper professional HR advice before "going legal"

→ Write up your own account of the interview as soon as possible after the interview

→ Take offers of feedback and listen well

W Workbook Supplement

Exercise 1:
Answering the basic questions

Where is my career going?

→ What chance do I *really* have at this upcoming interview?

→ Why have my previous interviews failed?

→ Do I know what makes me an effective performer at interview?

→ What will the interview achieve?

→ What is the Interviewer really looking for?

→ What will I get out of the interview — **whatever the result?**

Exercise 2:
REVIEWING your CAREER to date

Your Ultimate Career Goal	
Your role	
Level	
Salary	
Type of work you would like to be doing	
What will help me get there?	
What do I need to organise (training, development, experience etc.) to get me there?	

Exercise 3:
Review your last year at work: Major projects and achievements.

What did you do? What did you learn?

Quarter	Work	Learning New knowledge, skills, attributes
1		
2		
3		
4		

Exercise 4:
Matching your experience to Competencies

Start your own list... the first example is free!

Competency	Sample Questions	Proofs
Leadership	What experience do you have of leadership?	5 years in my current role —teams are typically 6- 10 persons; I led the team during this difficult situation...

Exercise 5:
PROMOTION INTERVIEWS:

New versus old Job –
What's the Overlap, What's the Difference?

KSAs = Knowledge, Skills, Attributes

	Current Job	Promotion
Common Items (KSAs)		
KSAs to be expanded by Re-training or other forms of learning		
New tasks on promotion		
Tasks to be left behind in going to new role		

Exercise 6:
IDENTIFY SUPPORT THAT YOU PROVIDE

What people rely on you in some way?	
For what do they rely on you?	
What skills or expertise are you using in supporting them?	

Exercise 7:
COMPLETING A 'PAR'

New versus old Job
What's the Overlap, What's the Difference?

P: PROBLEM Tell me about a problem that you had with a difficult client?	
A: ACTION What were the main actions that you took in that situation?	
R: RESULT What results did you achieve?	

Exercise 8:
COMPLETING A 'SPAR'

Practice your responses to having a problem thrown at you by completing the exercise below:

S: SITUATION Describe briefly a work situation from your recent past that you would like discussed at interview.	
T: TASK What were the challenges within the task and its context?	
A: ACTION What actions did I take? Why?	
R: RESULT What results did I achieve?	

Exercise 9:
Generic Questions:

If asked these at interview what would you say?

The Question	What You would say (in point form)
1 Tell me about yourself?	
2 What are your strengths?	
3 What are your weaknesses?	
4 What differentiates you from anybody else?	
5 Why should we give you the job?	

Exercise 9:
Generic Questions:

The Question	What You would say (in point form)
6 Why does this job interest you?	
7 What salary are you expecting?	
8 Where do you see yourself in five years' time?	
9 How would your colleagues describe you?	
10 Is there anything else you would like to add?	

Exercise 10:
PRESENTATION PREPARATION

At what level do the panel want me to pitch?	
How can I structure the presentation? BEG-MID-END	
How can I make my presentation impactful?	
What will I do to ensure that I relate well to the panel, and not to my visual aids?	
How will I groom?	
What does the Panel know/not know or understand? What unique information do I have? What is my objective?	

Exercise 11:
LAST MINUTE CHANGES

What last minute changes occur to you, or are prompted by some context change?

Are they worth making or will they interrupt my 'flow'?

If they are sufficiently important to include, how will I emphasise them?

Exercise 11:
Reviewing your last interview:

What Worked?
→
→
→
→
→
→

What needs fixing?
→
→
→
→
→
→

Notes

Notes